SHARING ECONOMY

GLOBAL CITIZENS: SOCIAL MEDIA

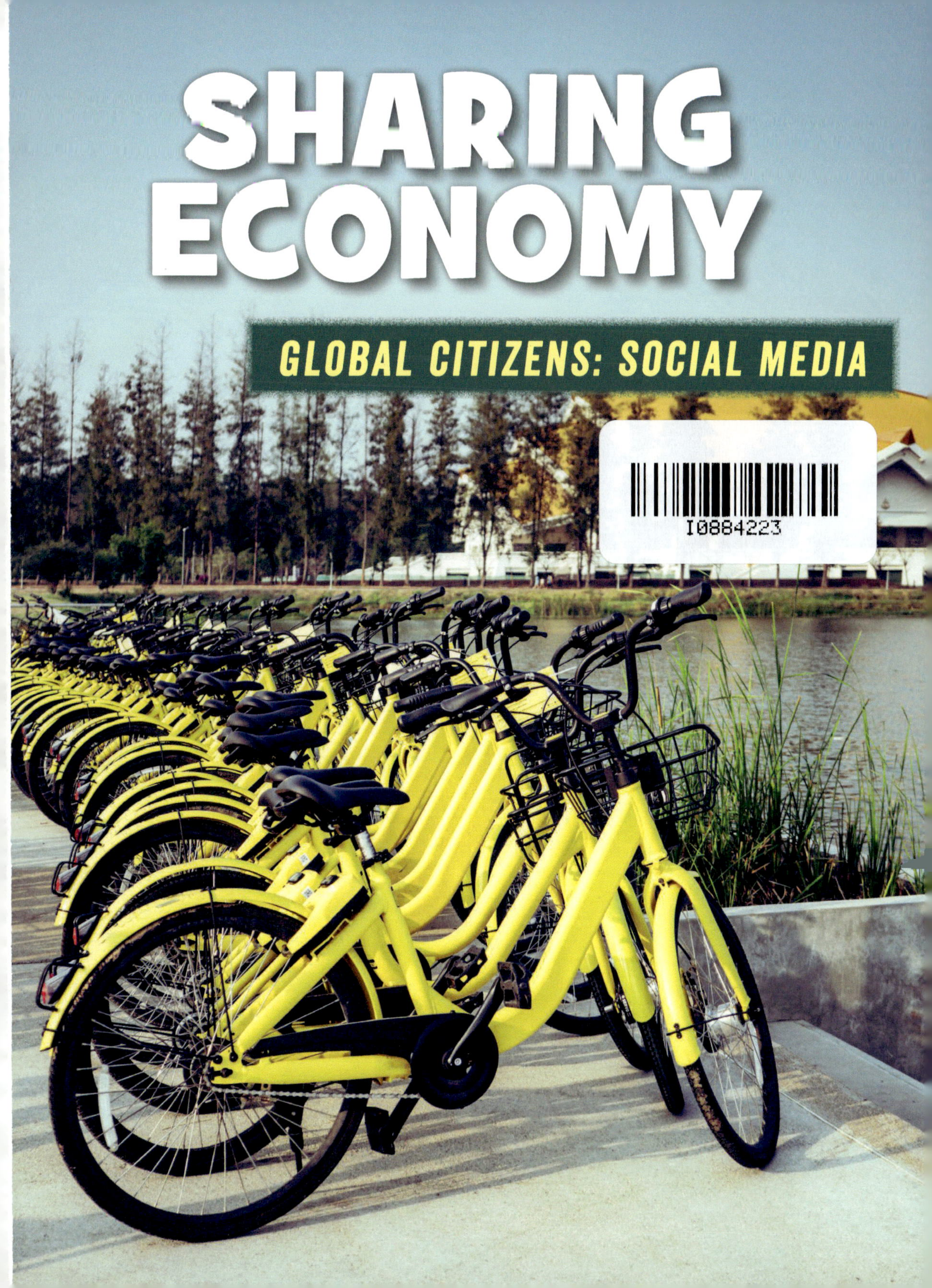

Published in the United States of America by Cherry Lake Publishing
Ann Arbor, Michigan
www.cherrylakepublishing.com

Content Adviser: Marcus Collins, MBA, Chief Consumer Connections Officer, Marketing Professor
Reading Adviser: Marla Conn MS, Ed., Literacy specialist, Read-Ability, Inc.

Photo Credits: © NatchaS/Shutterstock.com, Cover, 1; © Pack-Shot/Shutterstock.com, 5; © AlesiaKan/Shutterstock.com, 6; © All About Space/Shutterstock.com, 8; © wavebreakmedia/Shutterstock.com, 11; © imtmphoto/Shutterstock.com, 13; © slyellow/Shutterstock.com, 14; © Aaron Amat/Shutterstock.com, 17; © Monkey Business Images/Shutterstock.com, 19; © Karl_Sonnenberg/Shutterstock.com, 20; © Aila Images/Shutterstock.com, 23; © Hathaibunn/Shutterstock.com, 25; © sirtravelalot/Shutterstock.com, 26; © Tero Vesalainen/Shutterstock.com, 27; © dimmitrius/Shutterstock.com, 28

Library of Congress Cataloging-in-Publication Data

Names: Orr, Tamra, author.
Title: Sharing economy / Tamra B. Orr.
Description: [Ann Arbor, Michigan] : Cherry Lake Publishing, [2019] | Series: Global citizens: social media | Audience: Grade 4 to 6. | Includes bibliographical references and index.
Identifiers: LCCN 2018035593 | ISBN 9781534143111 (hardcover) | ISBN 9781534139671 (pbk.) | ISBN 9781534140875 (pdf) | ISBN 9781534142077 (hosted ebook)
Subjects: LCSH: Cooperation—Juvenile literature. | Sharing—Economic aspects—Juvenile literature. | Cooperation. sears
Classification: LCC HD295 .O637 2019 | DDC 302/.14—dc23
LC record available at https://lccn.loc.gov/2018035593

Cherry Lake Publishing would like to acknowledge the work of the Partnership for 21st Century Learning. Please visit www.p21.org for more information.

Printed in the United States of America
Corporate Graphics

ABOUT THE AUTHOR

Tamra Orr is the author of more than 500 nonfiction books for readers of all ages. A graduate of Ball State University, she now lives in the Pacific Northwest with her family. When she isn't writing books, she is either camping, reading, or on the computer researching the latest topic.

TABLE OF CONTENTS

CHAPTER 1

History: A Matter of Trust

Do you consider yourself a trustworthy person? Do you trust others easily?

Those two questions have never been more important than they are in today's **sharing economy**. The sharing economy is part of daily life. And it centers on trust.

Bartering, IOUs, and Sharing

Most economies tend to be based on a simple idea: you need something. Someone has it, and you have to find a way to get it. According to historians, past civilizations **bartered** for what they needed among people they didn't trust. With people they did trust, like those within their own community, these civilizations asked for goods or services with the understanding that the favor will

The ancient Maya civilization bartered with cocoa beans!

be returned at a later date. (This is known as a **gift economy**.) These civilizations relied on a system in which to get what they needed, they had to give something in return—either immediately or potentially at a later date.

Today, you most likely pay money in exchange for something you need. The sharing economy has a slightly different focus. You need something. Someone has it and doesn't use it very much. But instead of selling it to you, the person shares it for a reduced fee. Just a few years ago, today's methods of sharing items or services would have sounded unbelievable. Open your house to total

Airbnb is transforming the hotel industry.

strangers, or sleep in someone else's? Use your car as a taxi and drive strangers where they want to go, or willingly get into a stranger's car? Sounds dangerous! So why are companies like Airbnb and Uber, which provide these services, making billions? The answer? Social media.

No Longer Strangers

Before social media sites like Facebook and Twitter became popular, people weren't in the habit of sharing personal details online. In fact, you were warned against this. However, thanks to these social platforms, the concept of "stranger danger" is fading. You talk to people across the globe. You chat, seek advice, ask questions, and get to know one another without ever meeting. You can also share information, make suggestions, and offer opinions. Because of this social connectedness, the idea of a stranger renting out your extra room or riding in your car isn't odd—it's part of your daily life.

Timeline

Launch	Program or Company	What It Is ...
1965	Witte Fietsen (White Bikes)	Activists in Amsterdam left dozens of bikes unlocked for people to use
1995	Bycyklen (City Bikes)	Copenhagen bike-sharing program that uses a coin-operated system
1995	Craigslist	Website that lists jobs, housing, items for sale and wanted, etc.
2005	Etsy	Online shop that allows users to list and buy things like clothing, jewelry, or furniture
2008	Airbnb	Lease or rent short-term lodging
2009	Uber	Ride-sharing app
2012	Lyft	Ride-sharing app
2017	Bird	Electric scooter-sharing app
2017	Lime	Bicycle- and electric scooter-sharing app

According to a survey, about 470 million drivers would prefer to carpool.

To Recommend or Not to Recommend ...

Social media further helped the sharing economy gain popularity in a number of ways. Many platforms, like Airbnb and Uber, integrate social platforms, like Facebook, into theirs. This allows both renters and owners to check if they have friends in common. Social media creates trust by allowing and encouraging users to speak their mind. Users can review and rate their experience both on social media and on the company's website. This system of reviewing and rating a business helps businesses do better. It also helps customers choose wisely.

In a sharing economy, trust is essential and must be mutual. Sellers have to trust their customers, and customers have to trust the sellers. Almost all of that trust comes from participating in social media. People looking for products or services read reviews, compare prices, look at photos, and ask questions, all from behind their keyboards.

Developing Questions

Have you ever bartered anything? Or asked for a favor? It is a process that goes back centuries. "I will help you move that rock if you help me plow this field." "I will give you wheat, and you'll owe me later when I need help." Bartering and gift-giving is the foundation of the sharing economy. What are the advantages and disadvantages of bartering or asking for favors? Think of times when you've bartered or asked for a favor. Were both parties happy?

CHAPTER 2

Geography: Around the Globe

Sharing economy companies are found throughout the world. For instance, Uber has cars and drivers in 630 cities, 77 countries, and on 6 continents! In the United States, 75 percent of the country's population has access to its services. Airbnb has over 4 million listings in countries around the world. Let's take a closer look at other sharing services and products across the globe.

India and Dubai

In India and Dubai, consumers who need to rent household items or party supplies, like tents or speakers, turn to RentSher. RentSher does everything from photographing and listing the owner's equipment to transporting the items to the renter. RentSher makes the renting process the easiest it could be.

The sharing economy is defined differently in different countries. China includes Amazon and Netflix in the industry, whereas the United States doesn't.

Another Indian company, Ravgo, was created out of a need by poor farmers. Many farmers in India often need agricultural equipment for their crops but can rarely afford to buy these expensive machines. In 2016, Vikas Goyal launched Ravgo. The company matches people who own equipment with those who don't.

China

The largest sharing economy in the world is China. Like Uber in the United States, China has Didi Chuxing, a ride-sharing company. It started in 2011, and by 2015, it had provided over 1.4 billion rides in that year alone! Many Chinese passengers choose to carpool, saving gas and lessening the amounts of **carbon dioxide** in the air. China also has bike-sharing companies like Mobike and Ofo. Six million users jump on a bike, ride it, and then use the included lock to leave it wherever they want. A built-in GPS sensor records where it is left. In other Chinese cities, people can temporarily rent an umbrella or a basketball for shooting some hoops at the park!

About 50 percent of China uses a sharing economy platform.

Grab is known as the "Uber" of Southeast Asia.

Europe

From pets to food waste, the people and companies of Europe are all about sharing. DogBuddy has saved dog owners time and money in many countries, including Sweden, Germany, Italy, France, the United Kingdom, and Spain. Since launching in 2013, the platform has become one of the largest "dog sitters" in Europe. Owners can find dog sitters in their area and read reviews to find the best sitter.

Too Good To Go is another European platform. Launched in 2015, this Denmark-based company helps restaurants, bakeries, and cafes reduce food waste. At closing time, these businesses list leftover items on Too Good To Go that haven't sold and can't be sold the next day at a reduced price. Within 2 years, the app has saved over 2 million meals that would have otherwise been tossed out!

Gathering and Evaluating Sources

As pleased as many people are about the development of the sharing economy, there are some who are less than thrilled. Traditional taxi companies and hotel chains, for example, are not happy about these changes. When Uber launched its business in Europe, it was met with protests and even violence. In France, the head of Uber was arrested, and cars and tires were burned in city streets. Using the internet and your local library, research this topic further. Why do you think some traditional companies are upset over the success of sharing companies? Can you find other examples in which a sharing economy company disrupted a traditional company?

CHAPTER 3

Civics: Sharing Has Rules

More and more people have figured out that they can make money by offering their unused goods and services to the public. Consumers have realized how much money they can save by using sharing economy services.

Despite all the good that comes from a sharing economy, there are a growing number of legal issues. Giant businesses, like Uber and Airbnb, have had to figure out their share of them. For example, what happens if an Uber driver hits someone while taking a passenger to a destination? Or if someone staying in an Airbnb steals items from the home? Who is **liable**? These are questions that everyone from lawyers and judges to business owners and renters are trying to figure out.

According to a 2017 survey, only about 17 percent of adults are "very trusting" of certain services in the sharing economy.

Communications Decency Act

Currently many sharing economy businesses are using the Communications Decency Act of 1996 for protection. This law states that internet-based service providers are not liable for the words or actions of their users. Some people object to using this law for providers like Uber and Airbnb. Unlike people posting something on Twitter or Facebook, these companies are connecting people who otherwise would not have connected. They're bringing these people face-to-face in the real world.

Real Name Profiles

Trust is the key to a sharing economy, so individuals are expected to follow a real name system. They must create accounts or profiles based on their actual names, not nicknames or handles. In many cases, this means providing government-verified identification documents, like a passport or driver's license, in order to participate in a sharing platform. This helps weed out fake profiles.

Feastly and Eatwith are companies that allow users to dine in someone's home!

The sharing economy can also be good for our planet!

More Questions

Other problems with the sharing economy keep popping up. Ride-sharing businesses, like Uber and Lyft, have been involved in a lawsuit with the Disability Rights Advocates for not picking up disabled passengers or those with service dogs.

Airbnb and other home-sharing companies have problems as well. A number of neighborhoods around the country are complaining to their local leaders that they don't want homes near them being used as bed-and-breakfasts or hotels. Also, under federal civil rights laws, hotels and landlords cannot **discriminate** on the basis of race, gender, or religion. Should these rules apply to homeowners who are sharing their home? Hotels have to pay occupancy taxes and provide space for both abled and disabled people—should Airbnb hosts do the same?

As the economy changes, so will the regulations surrounding these changes. It is a growing process, and it is more than likely to have a lot of bumps and lawsuits in the process. As sharing economy writer Glenn Carter once stated, "There will be growing pains along the way—and more horror stories, no doubt—but the sharing economy is here to stay."

Developing Claims and Using Evidence

Look at the many different issues discussed in this chapter. Choose the one that is most interesting to you. Make a claim ("Uber drivers should always pick up disabled passengers" or "Airbnbs should not have to pay hotel-like taxes") and then gather evidence to support your claim. Think about why this issue is a problem in the first place. Try to see the problem from the viewpoint of each party involved. How do you feel about your claim when you have considered all of the evidence?

CHAPTER 4

Economics: Changing Attitudes

How do you make decisions about what to do, where to go, or what to buy? If you are like the majority of people, you rely on the opinion and recommendation of someone you know and trust.

Word of Mouth

According to research, more than 90 percent of people in 56 countries list "word-of-mouth" recommendations as the most influential advertising. Today, the majority of those recommendations are coming from social media sites. Your sister "pins" a beautiful shirt on Pinterest, and you end up buying one in another color. Your neighbor posts a negative review of a restaurant on his Facebook or Yelp profile, and you make a note to never eat there again.

Research predicts that the sharing economy industry will grow to $335 billion by 2025.

When it comes to companies that offer services in a sharing economy, almost 70 percent of people stated they would not trust the company until it was recommended by someone whose opinion they trust.

To Own or Not to Own

For many years, people have pushed to own things. The more you had, the more successful you were. This attitude is changing, especially for today's consumers between ages 18 and 24. They are streaming music and movies instead of buying CDs, DVDs, or downloading a digital copy to own. In 2017, there were more than 30 million people that paid for a music streaming service, like Spotify and Apple Music. These services make up about 62 percent of the entire U.S. music industry! Compare this to digital downloads, which were down 24 percent in 2017. Physical sales were also down. Many of these young consumers are also hopping in Ubers rather than buying cars and paying for insurance. This is especially true in larger cities like Los Angeles, California, and New York City, New York, where owning a car is more of a hassle and sometimes more expensive. In fact, in 2016 only 60 percent of 18-year-olds had a driver's license compared to 80 percent in the 1980s!

Communicating Conclusions

While there is little doubt that the sharing economy is going to grow over the next few years, there are questions about if this is an entirely positive step. After reading about the difficulty monitoring and creating laws for these businesses, and weighing that against the ease and convenience for people, which side of the debate do you agree with the most? Do you think the sharing economy should grow, or do you think it brings too many problems? Talk about this topic with family and friends. Are their opinions different based on their age or experience with the internet?

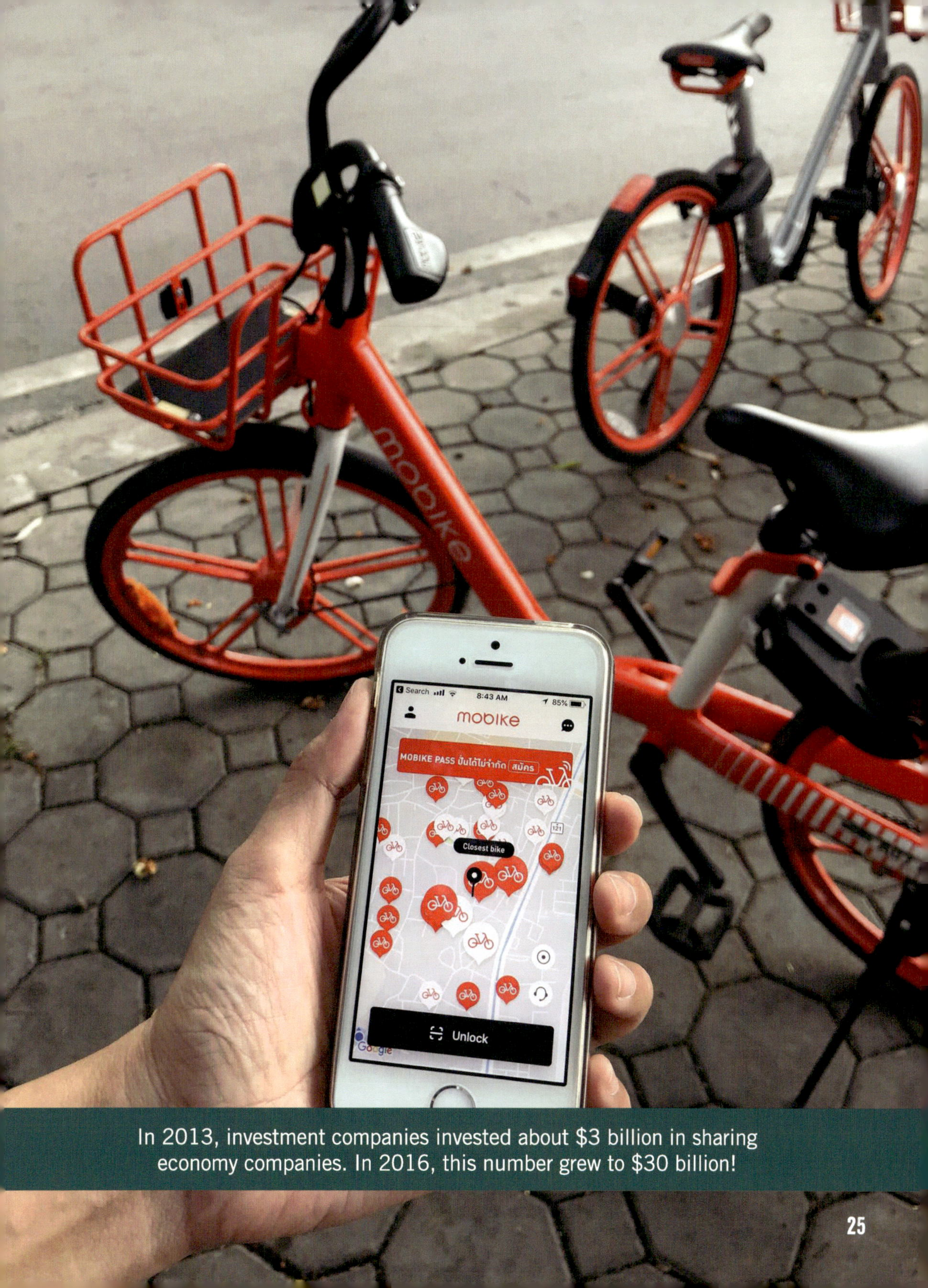

In 2013, investment companies invested about $3 billion in sharing economy companies. In 2016, this number grew to $30 billion!

According to studies, about 50 percent of adults will use Airbnb or a similar service during summer travel.

If you're sharing an Uber with family or friends, Uber allows you to seamlessly split the cost with up to three people!

Making Big Bucks

Airbnb, Uber, and Lyft are the three companies you most likely think of when someone mentions the sharing economy. Together, these three giants are worth more than the country of Morocco's entire economy! (This is also known as **GDP**.) Morocco's GDP in 2016 was a little over $103.6 billion, while Airbnb, Uber, and Lyft were worth about $106 billion!

Uber now features UberEATS, UberPOOL, and even UberKITTENS!

The three companies also employ a lot of people. Ride-sharing companies are quickly becoming the most popular way to earn extra cash. In 2017, Lyft had about 1.4 million drivers making, on average, about $377 a month. The 2 million Uber drivers were making about an extra $364 a month. And those who drive for both Uber and Lyft made slightly more each month, about $396 to $481. Airbnb, the other top sharing company, has connected more than 160 million guests to homes in 191 countries in 2018. The hosts on average took in about $924 extra a month.

Taking Informed Action

Have you ever looked around your room and thought, what am I not using? Are there clothes that are too small, books you've already read, or bicycles you don't ride? How about toys you have outgrown? Could any of them result in money? Brainstorm some ways you might be able to offer a product or service to others based on what you already own. Be creative—look around your house and discuss it with your parents. What can you come up with?

Think About It

According to a study, 21 percent of American adults—or 44.8 million—were using sharing economy services in 2016. The study predicts that, within the next few years, this number is going to rise to 38 percent or 86.5 million. How will this increase be reflected in the way people buy things? What impact will it have on businesses like hotel chains and taxi companies?

For More Information

FURTHER READING

Osalor, Peter. *Teenage Entrepreneurs: The Best Time to Start Your Own Business.* London: POSAG International, 2012.

Rankin, Kenrya. *Start It Up: The Complete Teen Business Guide to Turning Your Passions into Pay.* San Francisco: Zest Books, 2011.

Speights, Kevin. *Become a Teen Boss: 20+ Ways to Make Money Using Your Electronic Device!* Tampa, FL: Kiddie Mojo Publishing, 2015.

Sutherland, Adam. *Be a Young Entrepreneur: Be Inspired to Be a Business Whiz.* Hauppauge, NY: Barron's Educational Series, Inc., 2016.

WEBSITES

JustPark—The Most Popular Ideas in the Sharing Economy
www.justpark.com/creative/sharing-economy-index
Discover all the different types of sites and companies that offer shared services and products.

BookMooch
http://bookmooch.co.uk
Find out how you can share your books with others!

GLOSSARY

bartered (BAHR-turd) exchanged goods or services rather than paid for them

carbon dioxide (KAHR-buhn dye-AHK-side) a colorless, odorless gas

discriminate (dis-KRIM-uh-nate) to treat a group unfairly because of prejudice or bias

GDP (GEE DEE PEE) gross domestic product; refers to the size and value of all services and goods produced in a country over a specific period of time

gift economy (GIFT ih-KAH-nuh-mee) a system in which goods and services are given freely and not traded for something else

liable (LYE-uh-buhl) legally responsible

sharing economy (SHAIR-ing ih-KAH-nuh-mee) a system in which goods and services are shared between people, usually through the internet

INDEX